When Wildflowers Bloom

Himala Palni Kapur

BookLeaf Publishing

India | USA | UK

Presentation by *BookLeaf Publishing*

Web: www.bookleafpub.com

E-mail: info@bookleafpub.com

ISBN: 9789363311305

First edition 2024

Dedicated to the lost children of wonder,
trying to find their way home.

You are home.

ACKNOWLEDGEMENT

My heart is full of gratitude for the mountains of Uttarakhand and Himachal, which have always held me in the gentle embrace of their silence as rivers of inspiration flowed through me. Between these pages, you will find the scent of those mountains—wild earth, butterflies, bees, and fallen leaves.

Thanks to my husband, Shashank, who has always been a mountain of support. He has loved me at my best and held me at my worst. Thank you for being you.

A special thanks to Sushant, a brother from another mother and perhaps a piece of my soul. I am grateful for the warmth of your presence in my life.

I am eternally grateful to my parents, Lokman and Uma, for giving me a beautiful childhood in the mountains amidst the tall pines and the mighty deodars and for sowing the seed of appreciating and observing nature in its true and raw form within me.

Finally, to the verses between these pages. Thank you for choosing to flow through me.

PREFACE

As a child, I often found myself outside, in nature, quietly observing ladybugs, butterflies, flowers, and dew drops on leaves. I was an only child with both parents working, so I spent a fair share of time all by myself, doing nothing or thinking or observing. This time with myself has shaped who I am and taught me, very early on, the importance of solitude and of enjoying my own company. I'd often imagine myself as a being of magic, wondering about the mysteries of the world, and talking to birds, animals, mountains, and trees. I believed they could hear me as certain as I was that I could understand them.

When I was not outside being one with nature, I'd spend my time writing stories, painting, singing, and dreaming of being a writer, a painter, and a singer.

Then adulthood hit, and the fantasies of a child of wonder were crushed under its weight.

Though my imagination was still fertile and my faith that we are all connected still brimmed, something paused. I stopped being a writer, a painter, and a singer. I became what the world around me asked me to be, but somewhere, the dreamer was still alive. Then as I went through a series of heartbreaks, rebirths, personal traumas, rediscovering love and gratitude—the seed that had always been there slowly mustered the courage to sprout. The dreamer awoke.

'When Wildflowers Bloom' is the dream of the awakening. It is a poignant expression of that longing for connection, for simplicity, and for the quiet beauty that surrounds us.

It's a reminder to slow down, to appreciate the small miracles of nature, to live the magic of everyday life, and to find solace in solitude.

It's a wish. It's an affirmation. It's an invitation and a promise to never forget that child of wonder. So, leave behind the cacophony of the world and allow yourself to be enveloped by the quiet beauty of these verses.

Believe and you'll find magic in these pages.

A Picture of You

It takes a poem to tell the truth,
To paint a picture of you.

To describe the colour of your iris,
A blazing fired-yellow held by the brown, akin
to the dirt of the earth,
Floating in an ocean of crystal waters where,
Ever so often, a drop silently escapes the curves
of the Lacrima.

It takes a poem to tell the truth,
To paint a picture of you.

To describe the shape of your smile,
A gingival arch, unfurling the pink of spring,
A concave bow lighting up the creases of your
gleaming eyes,
Whilst a troop of whites stands guard.

It takes a poem to tell the truth,
To paint a picture of you.

To describe the canopy that veils the crown,
A black darker than the brushstroke of midnight,
Cascading in ebony tendrils of locks, curls,
spiral and twine,
Caressing the creases upon your forehead.

It takes a poem to tell the truth,
To paint a picture of you.

To describe the bridge upon your face,
A slender line of ancestry, of breath,
A contour of lineage and lore,
Like a sculpture carved by the hands of time.

It takes a poem to tell the truth,
To paint a picture of you.

To describe the brow upon your forehead,
A witness to the weight of worries,
A furrow holding sacred thoughts,
Like a sparse ridge on a mountaintop.

It takes a poem to tell the truth,
To paint a picture of you.

But to truly capture the incense of your essence,
I must traverse the labyrinth of your spirit,
Where laughter and sorrow walk hand in hand,
And shadows dance to the light of your soul.

And I realise,
It will take a symphony of words to convey,
The melody of your existence,
Where each note will be a reflection of your
being,
Rhyming with the rhythm of your heart.

And I realise,
To describe the depth of your gaze,
Is to dive into the abyss of your secrets,
Where galaxies collide and stars are born,
In the endless expanse of your cosmos.

And I realise,
It will take an epic to unravel,
The enigma of your thoughts,
Where dreams weave into reality,
And fantasies bloom in the garden of your mind.

And I wonder,
If a lifetime is enough to comprehend,
The intricacies of your existence,
For you are a mosaic of experiences,

A medley of love and longing.

And I realise,
It takes more than a poem,
More than words on a page,
To capture the truth of who you are,
For you are a masterpiece, an inconceivable
work of art.

I see you, twice

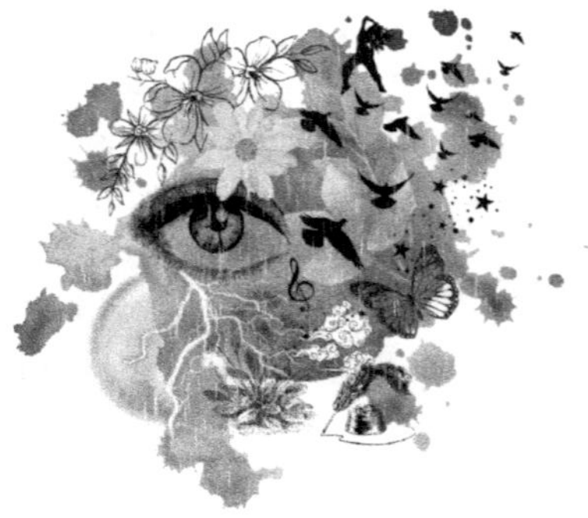

What if I told you I don't see you,
The way you seem to the world?

You are the lightning of a stormy night,
The spark igniting fires wild.

You are the earth beneath, the ether above,
The waters streaming from the skies.

You are the wind, whispering secrets of time,
A glowing orb, a strobe of light.

You are the smile of a little child,
The dreams, the colours in sparkling eyes.

You are the force of gravity,
A luminous embodiment of eternity.

You are a timeless song with a different melody,
Stardust and sand, a dose of ecstasy.

You are the dawn that breaks the longest night,
A phoenix rising, burning bright.

You are the echo of laughter in the rain,
A soothing balm to quiet the pain.

You are the rhythm of a heartbeat's quest,
A lullaby that brings sweet sweet rest.

You are the whisper of trees in the breeze,
A song, a melody of rustling leaves.

You are the pulse of the ocean's tide,
A force of nature, undefined.

You are the ink in a poet's pen,
The muse inspiring me again and again.

You are the silence in a crowded room,
The blossom in eternal bloom.

You are the thread that weaves through time,
A symphony, a celestial rhyme.

You are the light that never fades,
The essence of dreamy escapades.

You are the magic in the mundane,
Pure joy, like dancing in the rain.

You are the song of the universe's heart,
A magnificent, marvellous work of art.

So, will it be alright if I tell you I see you twice?
Once as the body, and once as the bearer of life.

Dear Beloved

I am certain we've already met in another form,
in another life.
I know this because I wait, carrying in my heart
a love that burns only for you.

And I wonder...

Which song speaks to you,
And do you discover yourself in its words every
time you listen to it?

Where do you wander in this vast world,
And what stirs the rhythm of your heart?

Do the mountains call to you like they do to me,
And does the wind, my emissary, bestow upon
your brow the tender kiss I send from afar?

Does the moonlight dance upon your bare skin,
Igniting flames of passion from another life and
another time?

Can you hear poetry in the whispering of trees,
And do you find solace in the warm womb of
the earth?

Have you witnessed dawn breaking over the
horizon,
And do you too find yourself floating in the
vivid colours of its brushstroke sky?

Do you lose yourself in the scent of wildflowers
carried by the breeze,
And can you taste its lingering sweetness like
nectar on parted lips?

I may not have seen you,
And yet your visage is set upon my eyes as if,
I've known you all my life and through all the
lives gone by,
And all the lives that lie ahead.

The ember of autumn promises your arrival,
And until that day comes, I wait,
Carrying in my heart a love that burns only for
you.

There you are

There you are..
Come to steal my peace.

Your beauty dives my thinking,
And I am slowly starting to believe..

You're the salt in the waters of my ocean,
And you're the friction in my every motion.

You're the honey dripping off my bare, naked
skin,
And you're the loud whispers on a quiet day's
end.

You're the melody of my darkest muse,
And you're the intoxication I cannot refuse.

You're the raw, primal scandal gliding down my
nape,
And you're the wildfire setting ablaze all my
escapes.

You're the thunder rumbling in the heart of my
bosom,
And you're the fracture within a chasm.

You're the beginning and end of all my desires,
O darling, you're the tempest brewing on
unbridled fires.

She was different, right?

A soft melody in the silence of night,
She was a guide to his soul's inner light.

With eyes, like windows to distant lands,
She was a secret only the heart understands.

Like lights, beaming through the darkest haze,
She was the sun, setting the horizon ablaze.

Fierce like a mother's tight embrace,
She was a wolf with a human face.

Untamed, wild, and free,
She was a symphony breezing through the trees.

Beneath the stars like the moonlight's quiet
escapades,
She was a lover's kiss wildly gliding down the
nape.

Like poetry, she kept his heart warm,
O, she was the calm after a violent storm.

Beautiful

I think my favourite word is "beautiful."
Ah! So simple, so common,
Yet perfect to describe a person, place, or thing,
And sometimes even a feeling.

"Aren't you beautiful!"
Akin to a silhouette gracing the canvas of the
setting sun.

"The melody of your voice is beautiful!"
Like the cadence of a mountain river cascading
towards the ocean.

"Your writing is beautiful!"
Like a tapestry woven with Rumi's pearls of
wisdom.

"The way you think is beautiful!"
Like birds gracefully circling the boundless
expanse of the cobalt blue skies.

"Your expression is beautiful!"
Intoxicating like the peacock dancing for the
rain.

"The yellow of your bare skin is beautiful!"
Like the caress of golden sunshine upon the
crest of the white snow-clad peaks.

"Your eyes, so deep and beautiful!"
Like the measure of the seven seas combined.

And I think, maybe, simple and common, is all
we need,
For within simplicity and the common,
Extraordinary beauty is waiting to be found.

Breath of my breath

I wish for you to see the mountains the way I see
them.

To listen to them and understand what they say
in their silence.

To wrap your arms around a rugged, mossy tree
and feel its heart beating against yours.

To take a dip in the cold waters of the wild river
and feel the lightness it brings, washing away
the burdens of this body and this life.

To hear the wind whispering in your ears, the
sacred secrets of ancestors gone and those yet to
arrive.

To feel the velvet of the dew-laden grass beneath
your feet and the warm kiss of the sun upon your
cheek.

To feel the pulse of the earth on your fingertips,
and know that you are part of something greater,
as the universe unfolds its script.

To bask in the beauty of the sunrise, painting the
sky with hues of gold, and let its warmth
envelop you as a new day unfolds.

To witness the stars dancing to the tune of the
moon's gentle lullaby, unveiling the magic of the
night sky.

To find solace in nature's embrace, and feel its
timeless wisdom in every moment, every place.

To lose yourself in the depth of its blue skies and
float away with the clouds to another universe,

Where you become the
— Breath of my breath,
— Bone of my bone,
— Flesh of my flesh.

What should I write about

Should I write about your smile,
Or about the depth of your eyes,
Or should I write about the melody of your
voice,
That dances to the tune of your fingers.

Should I write about that tiny speck on your
white shirt,
Or about the lines of destiny engraved on your
palms,
Should I write about that flirty curl of hair,
That sways with the wind gently teasing your
forehead.

Should I write a story of your innocence,
Or one, of your struggles,
Should I write anecdotes of your love,
That are still reminiscent in the air.

Should I write about your staying,
Or the story of your leaving,
Or should I write about the promises you made
aeons ago,
That have still kept me waiting.

Should I write tales of passionate love,
Or a narrative of the journey from 'we' to 'me',
Should I write about those dark and lonely
nights,
When even the moon, scared, hid behind a veil
of clouds.

Such was the spectacle of betrayal, of that
destruction,
Even the skies trembled in witness, and cried
frozen tears in spring,
The winds changed their direction,
And even the winter snow refused to touch that
mountain top.

So, now you tell me—
What should I write about?

Parallel Lines

So, we're like parallel lines.

Ever so close but never touching,
Side by side, yet never crossing.

Like yin and yang, two halves of a whole,
Like night and day, and the silent whispers of a
soul.

Engaged in a dance of shadows and light,
Like the stars in reflection, on a river, one
moonlit night.

Existing, breathing, and surviving under the
same sky,
Like a truth woven in a harmless lie.

Estranged with journeys entwined,
O darling, we're just like parallel lines.

You

Somewhere up in the skies,
With the stars I believe,
I dream of you often,
And every nocturnal visit is the same;
Of love and light.

Your smile,
Still as brilliant as the last time I saw you in
blood, bone and flesh.

Your voice,
Forever tender like the gentle breeze brushing
against my skin.

Your eyes,
Bright, staring into my soul, illuminating the
darkest recesses of me.

And as you sit beside me, in my dream,
A warmth much like that of the sun passes over
me.

You still feel so safe, as though with you by my
side,
No harm could come by and no storm could ever
touch me.

And words become obsolete, unnecessary,
For you possess an innate understanding, a silent
communion.

You navigate the labyrinth of my being
effortlessly,
As though I were an open book to your perusal,
Reading my every frown, smile and sigh, my
triggers, my relief and my release.

There is a picture of us, in a colourful frame
upon my table from over a decade ago.
I sometimes gaze at it,
Like a pilgrimage to old times,
Times of the same love and light.

Samsara

In the wee hours of a cold winter morning,
I left with a kiss you planted on my forehead.

That kiss, like a seed, took root within me,
Growing with each passing day.
Its roots delved deeper, coursing through my
veins,
Suffusing my mortal body with the warmth of
your love.

Then, one day, a beautiful yellow flower,
Emerged from the centre of my forehead,
Piercing through the pineal, and blossomed.

Oh, how it blossomed, spreading its sweet
fragrance far and wide.
My arms were its leaves, my torso its stalk.

Every now and then, the flower swayed with the
wind,
Dancing to the rhythm of life before it,
And soon forgot about the kiss that started it all.

Slowly, the sun drew nearer, scorching.
The leaves blistered,
And a few petals, singed by the heat, fell.
The stalk stood enduring the hot, dry summer in
the hope of better days.

The rains soon arrived, and it poured and
poured.
The petals and leaves grew heavy,
And as the stalk began to droop with all the
weight,
The flower affirmed for better days and sure
enough—

Autumn soon arrived, with all its hues of orange,
mustard, and brown.
The petals began to darken,
While the leaves readied to part with the stalk.
And as the last leaf fell and the petals withered
away,

The cold winter arrived.

The flower was gone, and so were the leaves.
The stalk remained looking brown and weak.
The petals that collected at the flower's feet
were now blanketed by the snow.
The bitter cold persisted until there was no sign
of the flower or the stalk.

Having forgotten its summer wrath,
And growing weary of the spectacle before it,
The sun inched closer each day,
Spreading its gentle golden, honey-dewed
warmth.

Before long, a beautiful yellow flower,
Emerged from the center of my forehead,
Piercing through the pineal, and blossomed once
more.

And as the flower began to sway with the wind,
Dancing to the rhythm of life before it,
The wise oak in the distance,
Which had witnessed many a winter go and
many a summer come by,
Smiled and said, 'Ah, here we go again!'

Daily reminders

Let the sun remind you that you have light
within,
No matter how dark it gets.

Let the moon remind you that you are whole,
No matter what phase you're in.

Let the trees remind you that the falling leaves,
Are a hope for spring.

Let the bird remind you that no matter how
melancholy the song,
There is wind beneath your wings.

Let the bee remind you that even if the flowers
are far and few,
There is a honeyed sweetness about home.

Let the squirrel remind you that no matter how
heavy the burden to carry,
There is stocked-up treasure waiting for winter.

Let the river remind you that no matter how
difficult the path,
The ocean belongs to her.

Let the winter remind you that no matter how
harsh it gets,
The snow will crack dormancy, and the seeds of
tomorrow will sprout.

Let the mountains remind you that no matter
how high you rise,
There is always a deep valley within to explore.

Let the night remind you that no matter how
dark it gets,
The stars are always shining.

Let the rains remind you that no matter how big
the storm,
There is always a reason to smile.

So, darling, the next time you feel down,
Read this again and remember that despite the
circumstances,
There is extraordinary beauty always waiting to
be found.

Elemental Love

There is romance in the trees,
Look how their flowers are curled in the leaves.

The rivers whisper sweet serenades,
As they carve through valleys and open glades.

The sun tenderly caresses the ocean's face,
Setting it ablaze with blushed golden grace.

The stars wink in a playful trance,
As the night sky begins its cosmic dance.

The moonlight dances on the lake,
Casting silver paths for lovers to take.

The clouds kiss the sky's blue expanse,
A gentle, slow, celestial romance.

The wildflowers sway, a flirtatious tease,
Inviting bees with perfumed ease.

The sand embraces the rolling tide,
In a dance where land and oceans collide.

The desert wind, with grains of gold,
Wraps the dunes in an ancient hold.

The geysers spout with fervent glee,
Proclaiming love of earth and sea.

The aurora paints the polar skies,
In fluorescent, shifting, glowing dyes.

From ancient stones to newborn springs,
Love is an eternal song that forever sings.

If you were here

O how beautiful it would be if you were here.

We'd lay under the night sky,
And I'd teach you to count the stars.

We'd chase butterflies together, and stop every
now and then to smell the flowers,
And maybe you'd bloom like a wildflower.

I'd show you the moon and the sun,
And maybe you'd learn to find beauty in the
mundane.

We'd make art every day,
And maybe you'd learn to fill your life with
colour.

We'd laugh and cry together,
And maybe you'd learn to feel and embrace
every moment.

I'd teach you to be alone and daydream,
And maybe you'd learn the importance of
solitude.

I'd teach you to speak life in rich vibrant colours,
And maybe beige wouldn't dare to touch you.

We'd look in the mirror and speak kind words,
And maybe you'd learn to forever know your
worth.

We'd sing for hours together,
And maybe you'd learn to move mountains with
your voice.

I'd talk about love ever so often,
And maybe crazy beautiful love is what your
heart would seek.

I'd teach you to say sorry when it is hard,
And maybe you'd learn to forgive others.

I'd leave you handwritten love notes on the wall,
And maybe affirmations would line the depths
of your soul.

I'd choose the uncomfortable and forever shake
up my ways,
And maybe you too would fight to live life bold
and brave.

I'd teach you to love and be kind to every life
form,
And maybe you'd learn the golden purpose of
life.

I'd tell you I love you a million times a day,
And maybe, just maybe you'd learn,
That even in my flaws, my lack and even in my
mistakes,
I gave you my entire heart, my beautiful child.

Maybe, that's why you are on my mind

I dreamt of you last night,
And in my sleep everything felt alright.
When I awoke, it felt sublime,
And maybe that's why you're on my mind.

Flipping through the pages of an old diary,
I found a dried out rose,
As I picked it up, a thousand memories flashed,
And maybe that's why you're on my mind.

Walking through the woods I asked you for a
sign,
A beautiful butterfly came by,
Settled on me and stayed for a while,
And maybe that's why you're on my mind.

Looking up at the night sky,
I saw a million stars.
One shone the brightest, I knew that was you,
And maybe that's why you're on my mind.

Seven coloured symphony

The afternoon arrived dressed in yellow,
And sang to the mighty trees in green.

The song was carried by the silver wind,
And delivered as a kiss on your pale-looking
skin.

The kiss tainted your cheek a blush red,
As your pink lips parted to whisper a name.

Upon hearing, the blue sky above turned grey,
And wept shimmering beads of rain.

Far far away where a lone river and mountains
meet,
Where skies are orange, violet, indigo and the
lands are forested green.

Carrying the song, a golden ray slowly emerged,
And waltzed with a falling drop of rain.

A lover's gaze caught the scene,
And as a symphony of seven colours played,

She finally remembered, love is the only thing
we carry,
As a quiet whisper or as a song blowing in the
wind.

Whispers of inquiry

A moment I know myself, and in the next, I
don't,
Like I am a fleeting thought within a thought.

Am I a continuous journey,
Or am I the stillness I perceive?

Am I the river flowing toward the ocean,
Or am I the ocean patiently awaiting the river's
arrival?

Perhaps I am akin to a dandelion, awaiting a
gust of wind,
Or am I the wind carrying the seeds of
tomorrow?

Could I be the boundless expanse of the sky,
Or am I the passing cloud traversing its
vastness?

Am I the marvel of water in a desert,
Or am I merely a shimmering illusion tempting
the thirsty seeker?

Am I an infinitesimally small part of the cosmos,
Or does the cosmos find its dwelling within me?

Am I this bone and flesh visible to the eye,
Or am I a subtle force of energy?

And if energy can neither be created nor
destroyed,
Whence do I originate, and where does my
journey lead?

Perhaps I am all these things and none at the
same time,
In a perpetual dance between,
– Knowing and unknowing,
– Learning and unlearning,
– Of being and becoming.

A moment I know myself, and in the next, I
don't,
Like I am a fleeting thought within a thought.

I'd Let You Know

Why do leaves fall and decay,
And why is autumn the journey home?
Where do the winds come from, where do they
blow?
If I knew this, I'd let you know.

Why did the earth part from its lover,
And is this why the sun burns for it so?
Did the blue above cry an ocean for the blue
below?
If I knew this, I'd let you know.

Why does the sky turn into a kaleidoscope of
colours,

And why do birds sing at twilight's glow?
Why does a river ceaselessly flow?
If I knew this, I'd let you know.

Why does the moon call upon the waves,
And why do stars light up the darkness aglow?
Why does light summon the shadows?
If I knew this, I'd let you know.

Why do mountains stand so silent,
And why does the forest breathe so deep?
Why does the heart yearn for a distant horizon?
If I knew this, I'd let you know.

Why do we dream of a world unseen,
And why laughter makes the spirit soar?
Why do tears fall in profound joy and deep
sorrow?
If I knew this, I'd let you know.

Why do we seek the meaning of life,
And why do questions lead to more?
Why do we wander, yet long for home?
If I knew this, I'd let you know.

Bubbles of soapy water

In the quiet of one sunlit afternoon,
I blew bubbles of soapy water.
And as the sunlight gently brushed against them,
Their ethereal iridescence shimmered.

Hues of purple, pink, and blue,
Danced with yellow, orange, and green,
In a kaleidoscope of colours,
Swirling, twirling, waltzing with the gentle
breeze.

Oh, how magnificently beautiful and delicate,
Were those bubbles of soapy water.
But to touch them meant their demise,
So, I stood, witnessing the play of the sun, wind
and water.

And with every passing moment, I knew their
end was near,
With bated breath, I watched each bubble burst,
Into a myriad of tiny droplets, each still whole,
And carrying within it the same ethereal,
iridescent shimmer.

And as the final bubble vanished into the ether,
I beheld a transcendent revelation:
Like iridescent droplets, we emerge from the
cosmic bubble,
Each a mirror of the whole, each the eternal
light's shimmering reflection.

And so, I now ask you,
Have you ever blown bubbles of soapy water?
Have you felt them come alive, imbued with
your breath of life?
Have you, on their fragile surface, seen your
own reflection?
And have you ever admired their beautiful
perfection?

And if you haven't, come, in the quiet of one
sunlit afternoon,
To blow bubbles of soapy water.

To discover, to celebrate your shimmering
iridescent soul,
To know you are forever whole.

Along the path

The curvy road was my companion,
And the mountains a constant guide,
The sun was a beacon of hope,
And the moon, a guiding light.

Then, one day, along came a lonesome dog,
And began following me,
We played for a while, shared some food,
And he walked a few miles with me.

At the bend, I found a fallen bird,
So I picked her up and carried her with me,
As time went by, she became strong,
And sang sweet melodies to me.

In the distance, I saw a tall tree,
Calling and beckoning me,
And when I came close, I saw,
Its red blossoms had carpeted the path for me.

I came upon a tattered house,
With smoke blowing from its chimney,
A family of three lived there,
And they graciously offered me some tea.

I walked and walked and walked some more,
Finding the skies above always shielding me,
When I got tired, a beautiful butterfly alighted,
And, for a short while, settled on me.

The leaves rustled, wildflowers danced,
And along came a buzzing bee,
Ah, the noisy woodpecker in the distance;
They were all companions to me.

Some friendships endured the test of time,
While some walked alongside only briefly,
A few lovers came by,
Some I left behind, and some left me.

In this journey called life,
I sometimes found myself alone but never quite
lonely,

And every time someone came along, even if
just for a while,
The journey became about 'us' and not just me.

So, when I say I am enough,
No, I am not closing my doors to intimacy.
I am rather making myself whole,
Inviting in kindred spirits on this shared path of
self-discovery.

In the end, I realise, each encounter, no matter
how brief,
Added depth to the narrative of this beautiful
journey.

Right person, wrong time

Right person, wrong time,
Let's understand this paradigm.
But before that, make no mistake,
In understanding that the universe makes no
mistakes.

With keen observation, we come to find,
The notion of wrong timing, a construct of the
mind.
For each one we meet is part of the plan,
Guided by forces beyond what we understand.

Though patience may wane and doubts may
arise,
The universe conspires, to our surprise.

In the canvas of life, each colour finds its
rightful place,
Revealing the magic of the universe's grace.

So, embrace the paradox and this rhyme,
For in the scheme of things, it's always the right
time.
Though paths diverge and tears may fall,
The universe, in its wisdom, knows it all.

Dirty nails

Why are your nails so dirty?

Because I,
Have been putting my hands in the earth,
In hope that it would take me.
You see, I have been shedding a lot lately,
I don't fancy a shovel, and I have no time for a
wash.

And I,
Have been digging graves,
For old versions of me.
The ones that have done their work,
The ones I no longer need.

And I,
Have been scratching the barks of trees,
Because the backs of lovers feel like
chalkboards,
Screeching and noisy, sending shivers down my
spine.

And I,
Have been gardening,
Planting seeds of wildflowers in the topsoil,
Fed by those dead parts of me,
The old versions of me.

And I,
Have been feeling the earth,
Lying on the dirt, grabbing it with bare hands.
And like I said, I have been shedding a lot lately,
I don't fancy a shovel, and I have no time for a
wash.

That's why you see, my nails are dirty.

Skyward reveries

I look at you, looking up high,
Finding shapes in the cotton-candied sky.

A stallion emerges, to be swiftly swept away by
the wind,
The sun's rays trailing its tail's fag end.

A fish appears and quickly swims across,
Creating ripples through the clouds.

It is funny how the 'now' soon turns into an
illusion,
Or is it the illusion that becomes the reality of
now?

Time, like a master, has us on a hamster wheel,
Or maybe we've all got it wrong, and time really
isn't real.

Is it courageous to ride the tumultuous tides of
life,
Or is it okay to say, "I've had enough, I am
stepping aside"?

Why am I here? What purpose do I serve?
Or is the real purpose of life to 'simply exist,' to
'observe'?

I look at you, looking up at the sky,
As if uncovering the truth from under a blanket
of lies.

I look at you, looking up high,
A smile slowly appears as you breathe out a
sigh.

You turn to me and whisper, "Love is the answer
to the world,"
And in simple existence, its magic is unfurled.

Hello!

Hello, darkest parts of me!
Tonight, we will sit together again,
I will light a candle and graciously invite you in.

Hello, darkest parts of me!
Tonight, you will not be labelled 'sin'.
We will sit and have conversations and no one
has to win.

Hello, darkest parts of me!
Tonight, we will cry a few tears,
In silence, we face each other witnessing our
fears.

Hello, darkest parts of me!
Tonight, we will dance with the shadows,
Mirroring, touching, heart to heart, and toes on
top of toes.

Hello, darkest parts of me!
Tonight, we will melt into each other,
A promise to never confine you to a deep, dark
corner.

Hello, darkest parts of me!
I have lifted the veil and pulled back the curtains
today.
The stage is now set to showcase shadow's play.

Books on shelves

We are taught to weave the tapestry of life,
With a loom of fear and threads of sacrifice.

From birth, we learn to put others first,
Yet within, our own worth craves to be nursed.

Conditioned to give until we bleed,
Applauded for compromise and branded a traitor
if we choose to leave.

Caught in this cycle, we often find,
Our own hearts broken and left behind.

Addictions grip us, traumas repeat,
As we struggle to find solid ground beneath our
feet.

No one taught us to love ourselves,
And to place our hearts high, like books on
shelves.

Yet in the depths of our darkest despair,
A whisper lovingly lingers in the air.

"I love you, but I love me more,"
A declaration of a heart ready to heal, to soar.

For in this simple phrase you'll find,
A superpower, strong, compassionate, and kind.

To honor the self and set boundaries anew,
Embracing your worth, letting true love brew.

And it isn't selfishness, but self-care,
A choice we make to breathe in fresh air.

For only when I am whole and to myself true,
Can I extend my hand in true love to you.

So, choose to honour and love yourself,
To place your heart high, like books on shelves.

Circus of Life

I see you blowing rings of smoke,
Each bigger than the one before,
Hoping the tiger would jump through them,
And the circus will continue its show.

But the tiger doesn't dare.
He sits beside you, watching the rings float by,
Hoping one day he'll find the courage,
To leap through the rings of smoke you blow.

And I watch you both from a distance,
In a circus gone wrong,
Where the ringmaster lies in deep slumber,
And the tiger has been unsure for far too long.

The big top still hangs,
With ropes that are now frayed and worn,
A melancholy spectacle continues,
Of a dream that's forgotten and torn.

Do nothing, just let the music play,
And the spotlight shine bright,
For waiting is the greatest act of all,
In this circus called life.

The inertia will break,
For there is always a spark that refuses to die,
And when the tiger begins pacing his cage,
The ringmaster will awaken and rise.

The show will commence anew,
As rhythm begins to pulse,
The tiger will find the courage,
To leap through the rings of smoke.

Day and night

We journey through emotions, both dark and
bright,
Of pleasure and pain like the complexities of
day and night.

Some days, the pain feels like a lover's embrace,
Drawing us into its depths with gentle grace.

To romanticise pain is to lose sight,
Of the truth that keeps us anchored in the dark
night.

Acknowledging the depths of our soul's cry,
Forbids pain from soaring too high.

Acceptance must be our guiding light,
An anchor in the storms of our plight.

And, in the midst of this intricate dance,
Seekers find a balance, a delicate trance.

Dreamer and realist, hand in hand,
Navigating the shifting sands.

For only then can we hope to seek,
Peace amidst the pain we meet.

And in this balance, we find our way,
Through the complexities of night and day.

Wild child

O wild child,
With a gypsy soul,
You are flowers and fire,
With a river's roar.

You are mystery and marvel,
A song of the divine,
A child of the universe,
Come, stay a while.

Run free amongst the trees,
Listening to the wind,
Dance to the songs in your heart,
For you have stars within.

Laugh with the morning sun,
And in your eyes, hold the night,
Wander free through life's endless maze,
For you are a beacon of pure light.

Whisper secrets to the moon,
And dreams to the open sea,
In every step, hold a rhythm true,
For your heart is unbridled and free.

Embrace the storms that shape your path,
And cherish every scar,
For in your soul, a story lives,
As boundless as the stars.

O wild child, never tame,
Let your spirit soar,
For in your wanderings, you'll discover,
A love that truly endures.

O wild child,
With a gypsy soul,
Never forget, you are flowers and fire,
With a river's roar.

O Mother

In another universe, I met my mother who was
then a child,
Her smile innocent and her spirit free and wild.

I held her hand as we walked through a field of
wildflowers,
Excited, she named all the colours she saw and
often chased bees and butterflies.

We lay on the green meadow and looked up
high,
She marvelled at a flock of birds gracefully
circling the sky.

Then, in the cotton clouds, she spotted a horse
and a man in a cape,
Eyes gleaming with wild imagination, she
painted dreamy landscapes.

We came upon a river meandering through the
trees,
I took off her sandals and she dipped her tiny
feet.

She splished and splashed while a school of fish
circled a rock nearby,
Her little feet creating ripples that went far and
wide.

As the sun began to set, the sky turned to gold,
The birds returned to their nests, singing
melodies old.

A sparkle of fireflies emerged, o what a
twinkling sight,
In wonder, she beheld the magic of night.

She giggled as one came and rested on her little
nose,
Her laughter was a symphony, a sound I longed
to hold close.

In that dream, she remained a child, so free and
wild,
Her eyes sparkled with curiosity, her spirit
undefiled.

I watched her dance and twirl, lost in her own
world,
And I wondered what happened as life unfurled.

What trials and tribulations did she face that
made her so stern?
What dreams did she abandon? What lessons did
she learn?

In this waking life, I see a woman worn by
years,
Eyes of doubt and soul chained with fears.

Yet here, in this dream, she is untouched by
strife,
A reminder of the pure, unburdened joy of life.

I wish I could bring back the child within her
soul,
To mend the parts of her that life's hardships
stole.

And from this universe's embrace,

To the waking, I carry her essence, her joy, and
her grace.

For in this universe, she will always be a child,
With a spirit that is forever free and wild.

The greatest love of life

The greatest love of life,
It seems easily lost,
In the whirlwind of adulting,
Where bills loom and tidiness vies.

In duties and responsibilities,
Between compromise, sacrifice, and in being
nice.
The greatest love, often misplaced, we find,
Amidst the rush, a child's voice denied.

Yet within us, that spirit survives,
In dreams that shimmer and hopes that rise.
In skipping puddles, painting skies,
Proofing poems and seeking ties.

In the gentle touch of the wind's sigh,
In the wish on a lash, hoping it reaches the sky.
In blowing on a dandelion, letting desires fly,
Hoping one day the universe will comply.

Amid plans we doubt and dreams we seed,
In the quest for four-leafed clovers, that spirit is
freed.
The child of wonder emerges again,
Awake from its slumber, with its heart
unburdened and unchained.

So, let's pause amidst life's grand parade,
Embrace the magic, the child of wonder made.
For in these moments, we truly find,
The greatest love of life, the heart, the inner
child.

Children of wonder

We were not meant to be dazed by life's
sunshine,
Or to relentlessly stand under pouring rain and
thunderous skies.
No, we were not meant to turn our gaze away,
Or let the world's noises drown us alive.

We were not meant to let dreams remain dreams,
Or to annihilate the breath of the inner child.
No, we were not meant to be sculptures standing
still,
Or to allow violations to tear us apart.

We were meant to be astonished,
To be children of wonder.
Beings of magic,
To transform, transmute and not fluster.

We were not meant to burn,
But to be the fire,
Not to drown,
But to find the depth of our ocean.

We were not meant to be buried,
But to be vessels to hold,
Not to be blown away,
But to be the winding, whispering, gusting wind.

We were meant to waltz with the storm,
To find beauty in the chaos and grace in the fall.
We were meant to rise from the ashes,
A Phoenix, renewed and reborn.

We were meant to sing our own songs,
To let our voices echo through generations to
come and generations gone.
We were meant to love fiercely,
To nurture the gardens of our hearts and souls.

We were meant to walk with the shadows,
To chase the stars and dance in the moonlight.
No, we were not meant to be mere survivors,
We were meant to be the architects of life,
– to thrive,

– to shine,
– to be alive.

Unspoken burdens

I was aware of the pain you could cause me,
Yet I chose love to set me free.
For the regret of never loving, was a burden too great,
And I knew this could not be my fate.

You see, regrets, like shadows, in the silence they creep,
Unspoken burdens, they thrive in the heart's silent keep.
They linger like ghosts in the corridors of time,
Whispering of the forsaken self, like a rattling chime.

Like a silent aneurysm, regret bleeds you into
nothingness,
Slowly lowering you into the dark, suffocating
abyss.
Its tendrils reach, casting shadows deep,
A spectre haunting, a shackled heart, its keep.

In my narrative, regrets' face will remain unseen,
Detangling the web of 'could have beens.'
For I have found the strength to write my own
story bold,
And regrets will have no place as each tale I
carefully mould.

So, when I chose to love,
Aware of the pain you could cause me,
I was not weak in my plight, you see.
For, in choosing you, I was only choosing me.

Dancing with shadows

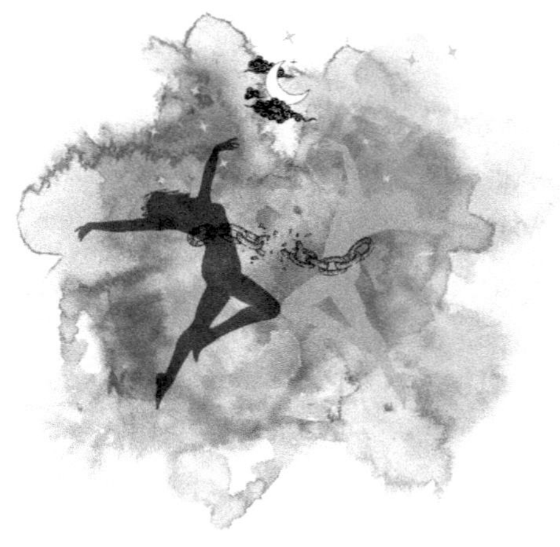

On a moonlit night she tore off her clothes,
Till there was no flesh and no bones.

Stripped of illusions, embraced by the night,
Her soul shone with its ethereal light.

She danced with shadows, a solitary waltz,
Each movement—a story, her heart's exalt.

She, a ballad, sung by the night,
A spirit liberating, taking flight.

Each step a defiance, against chains unseen,
In the moon's embrace, spirit reigned supreme.

Cloaked in the silence, yet speaking loud,
She painted her story in a moonlit shroud.

A melody of freedom in each daring step,
Lost in the rhythm, buried emotions crept.

The night bears witness to her silent cry,
A journey of discovery, reaching for the sky.

In the embrace of darkness, she found grace,
A soul was unbound, in this sacred space.

A sweet, sweet life

What a sweet, sweet life it would be,

To live for sunrises and sunsets,
Gazing in wonder as colours of twilight set.

To bathe in the silver light of the moon,
On star-studded, magical nights of June.

Go foraging in the forest for wild berries,
And build tiny homes in tree trunks for fairies.

To sip the elixir of the mountain streams,
And exchange flowers for wild honey from the
bees.

Cleanse our souls with the cold falling rain,
And dry them off with the warm summer breeze.

Weave tales of passion with the rustling leaves,
And dance in the shadows of ancient trees.

Trace constellations with our fingers pointing
high,
Lying under the canvas of a boundless sky.

With arms wide open, run through the tall grass,
And walk barefoot on moss-covered paths.

Count the stars with eyes brighter than summer
skies,
And witness the ceremonial dance of the
fireflies.

Hum to the tune of the westerly winds,
Joining in the song of the birds at a day's end.

The Call

When a birdsong inspires you to sing, sing,
Or if the butterfly beckons, spread your wings.

When the landscape calls, brush its colours
bright,
When your waking dreams, lean close, listen in
delight.

Perfect or flawed, answer the call,
In the song of the bird, in the flight of the small.

In a painting or in the dreams that enthral,
Do it all, for this is the call.

If lost, go back to your childhood, to guide your
way,
To those passions that fuelled your earliest days.

To the moments that sparked the innocent muse,
For this is the call you must never refuse.

Embrace the terror, and beauty alike,
Face the fear with courage, let passions ignite.

Whether wealth comes or not, or fame is a
fleeting sight,
Do it, for this is the call of your life.

Let your heart guide you, through shadows and
light,
In the imperfect, you are perfectly right.

For the bird and the butterfly, the canvas, the
dream,
All call out to you, to life's flowing stream.

Answer with courage, with love, and with grace,
For in each call you answer, you find your true
place.

Sing, fly, paint, dream, no matter how small,
For in each of these, you heed the call.

A place called home

I love to sit in solitude,
In a place that feels like home.
A place where the songs of the birds resound,
And humming winds blow.

A place where the trees know me,
And all the words my heart has poured.
A place where wildflowers bloom,
And is busy with butterflies and bees.

A place where the bull bellows,
And the beetles mellifluously whistle.
A place where dewdrops glisten,
And green grass always grows.

A place where cowbells ring,
And beyond the clouds, the skies are always
blue.
A place that is a pilgrimage,
And has buried the stories of many souls.

A place where sunsets are orange, pink, and
purple,
And the moonlight dances in a misty haze.
A place riddled with deep valleys,
Where waters gently flow.

A place where critters banter,
When the monsoon rains pour.
A place freckled with Rhododendrons,
And where a lone woodpecker's taps echo.

A place where winter settles,
And the autumn leaves whisper of the coming
snow.
A place where the mountains bow in salutation,
For their daughter has finally come home.

The Un-orphaned Orphan

He is a troubled child, they said,
Always up to some mischief.
Found in dark and untrusting places,
Places his innocent eyes should never have
glimpsed.

He is a troubled child, they said,
A victim of circumstances.
Those that should have kept him safe,
Had carved a life for him so wretched.

He is a troubled child, they said,
Unborn, abandoned by his father.
And then at birth, the mother fled,
For she was a child herself, all of just sixteen.

He is a troubled child, they said,
Raised and nurtured by his granny.
And then at thirteen, when he came of age,
He found himself in another grim quandary.

He learnt of his two brothers, they said,
One of blood and one born to another mother.
Whole, complete, with life full to the brim,
They were safe and shielded from every season's
weather.

It was a blow to his chest, they said,
A gaping hole punched through his gut.
He bled in silent solitude,
Distraught, broken with his heart in constant
torment.

And then the drinking began, they said,
A season of drowning out the world.
For it no longer was a place safe enough,
To shield him from the life ahead.

He is a rebel, a total trouble, that boy, they said,
He only keeps bad company.
With a gun in his pocket and a punch on his
knuckle,
His views on life are shrouded in a smoky haze.

That boy is trouble, they said,
When he was just trying to survive.
To find a place in a world that had no place for
him,
For even a mother's true love to him was denied.

That boy is trouble, they said,
To the man who came to his rescue.
And there, temporarily, he found,
A refuge from his disdain.

The world suddenly became beautiful, he said,
There was promise in the air.
A life dedicated to divine service,
Was going to be his fate.

That man tried, he said,
To help him find his ground.
But was it too late to make amends?
For the reality of his own existence, plagued the
boy's mind.

Then came along a girl, he said,
Who gave him her entire heart.
He carried it safely in his palms,
Till slowly the ghost from his past came
haunting back.

A decade and to be married, he said,

But he had witnessed so much dark.
He was modelled only broken relationships,
So how could he trust this new start.

So he let her go, they said,
Only to drown himself again.
The drinking and recklessness ensued,
Until he gave up on life and let it fade.

That man is trouble, they said,
He is never up to any good.
Little did they know of the battles he fought,
Just to keep himself afloat.

That man is trouble, they said,
Always on the run.
He chooses only the broken,
Feeding the demon of abandonment within, with
each broken one.

He drank and drank and then drank some more,
Till his eyes were finally sore.
Everyday ended just the same,
As hopelessness and despair filled his very core.

If only he'd look past this, she said,
He has the most beautiful soul.
A child just looking for love in the wrong
places,

A child who is still so unsure.

If only he would choose to transmute the pain,
she said,
And not drown in his sorrys and sorrows.
There was a life of promise waiting for him,
And so she prayed, he would choose to
metamorphose.

I'll write poems for him, she said,
And maybe, just maybe through them, he'll find
his release.
The demons he's been fighting for years,
Will finally leave and set him free.

I'll write songs for him, she said,
And perhaps he would shed his old skin.
Each musical note like a gentle breeze,
Would sweep away burdens and free him from
within.

She tried and tried and tried some more,
And just when she thought she couldn't
anymore,
He picked himself up and decided,
He couldn't take it a minute more.

He transformed his life, they said,
Became the best version of himself.

He finally found all the missing pieces,
And built a life full of hope.

He worked on himself, they said,
Threw that damned bottle out.
He chose to finally forgive himself,
And with that, his closure was found.

He lived happily ever after, he said,
For within himself all the answers he found.
He finally made peace with his heart,
And realised the love he deserved was within
him after all.

Sometimes we view life as victims, he said,
That realisation was his turning point.
He learnt to breathe through that gaping hole,
And finally mastered the art of life.

He lived on and shared his wisdom,
Gathered from far and wide.
The broken sought him, drawn to his light,
For he had overcome great darkness and was
now the guide.

Say Earth

Say, Earth, my hands were once muddy too,
And eyes maroon with blood.
I had the ravens' wings on my back,
And the antlers of a great stag on my head.

My face was of a mother bear,
And the belly of a great red sow.
My head was in the light of the sun,
And feet in the darkness below.

Say, Earth, I once sang with you,
To meet with the sky above.
My waters, lonely and deep,
Cried in longing to the stars above.

Say, Earth, I once was ether, with a blazing fire
in my chest,
I was the vast waters, the perfume of the wind.
I tread the path of lightning and rain,
The bridge between pleasure, sorrow, and pain.

I journeyed to the spirits' lair,
To seek visions the cosmos shared.
A guardian of balance, keeper of lore,
I spoke the language of the wind and stone.

I walked the waking and traversed the dreams,
I saw tales born out of shadowed schemes.
I inquired with the stars of hopes and fears,
That were answered in the language of silent
tears.

Say, Earth, I am the embodiment of all that is,
Bound by neither time nor space.
A vessel of existence, both eternal and fleeting,
I am the shaman, the walker of breath, death and
the in-between.

The grace of human race

The lines of time etched on your skin.
The mark of rain upon a human face.
The sensuous task of holding a perfumed kiss.
The embrace of hand.
The victory of an ordinary day.
The breath filling the hollow of a chest.
The feet holding the weight of mortality.
The beads of labour glistening upon a forehead.
The dirt trapped in the nails.
The musk of human scent.
The ache of unspoken words.
The relentless tide of time's advance.
The burdens of unshed sorrows.
The piercing shards of a broken heart.
The weariness of unending battles.
The longing for connection in a fractured world.

The vagueness of the void.
The weight of expectations never met.
The laughter that follows tears.
The whispering shadows.
The grief, the sorrow, the joy of tomorrow.
The forest, the sun, the roaring wind.

This is the grace of the human race,
Of love with all its trials, pains and bliss.

Defining the Undefinable

How does one define that which defies definite
definition?

How can one describe the earth,
Without invoking the verdant expanse of grass
and trees,
Or the boundless sky that weeps for it?

How does one omit the ocean that cradles its
curves,
The mountains that crown its crest,
The glistening glaciers,
And the rivers that etch their paths upon its
form?

How can one forget the birds whose melodies
grace dusk and dawn,
The critters and their playful discourse,
The wild beasts whose roars echo across its
breadth,
Or the wind whispering its eternal song?

How can one not allude to the sweet scent of
wildflowers,
And the buzzing of the bees,
The dirt beneath our feet,
And the rustling leaves?

How does one define that which is both simple
and complex,
The embodiment of the eternal,
The essence of the sublime,
The poetry of the universe?

How does one define that delicate dance
between—
The effable and the ineffable,
The tangible and the intangible,
The finite and the infinite,
The visible and the invisible,
The seen and the unseen,
The now and the forever,
Flowing in a timeless circle through time?

How does one define the breath of the breath of
the breath,
The song of being and becoming,
The subtlety of 'me' to 'we'?

How does one define love?